IISBN-13: 978-1720591344
ISBN-10: 1720591342

www.facebook.com/DeaBernadette

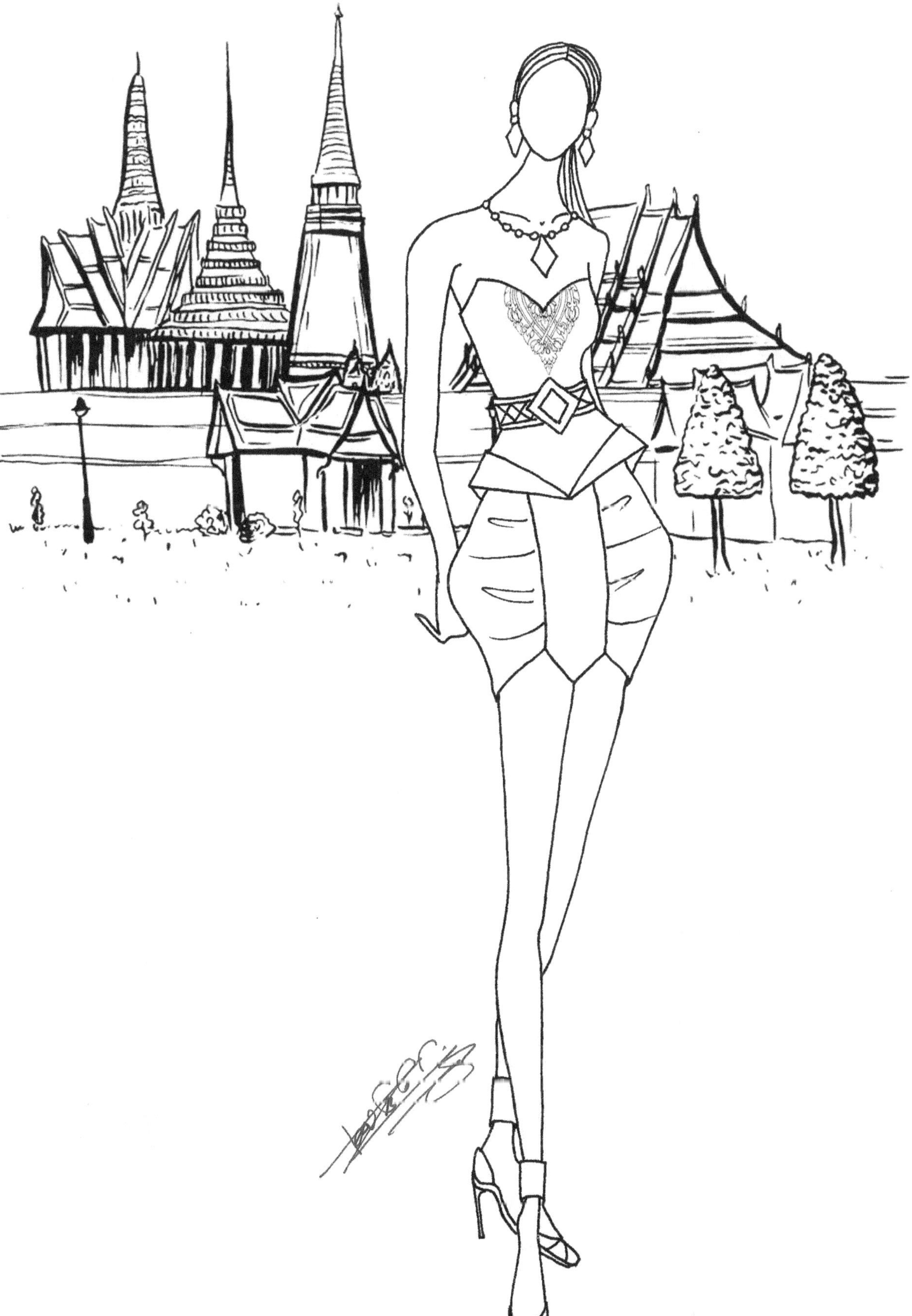

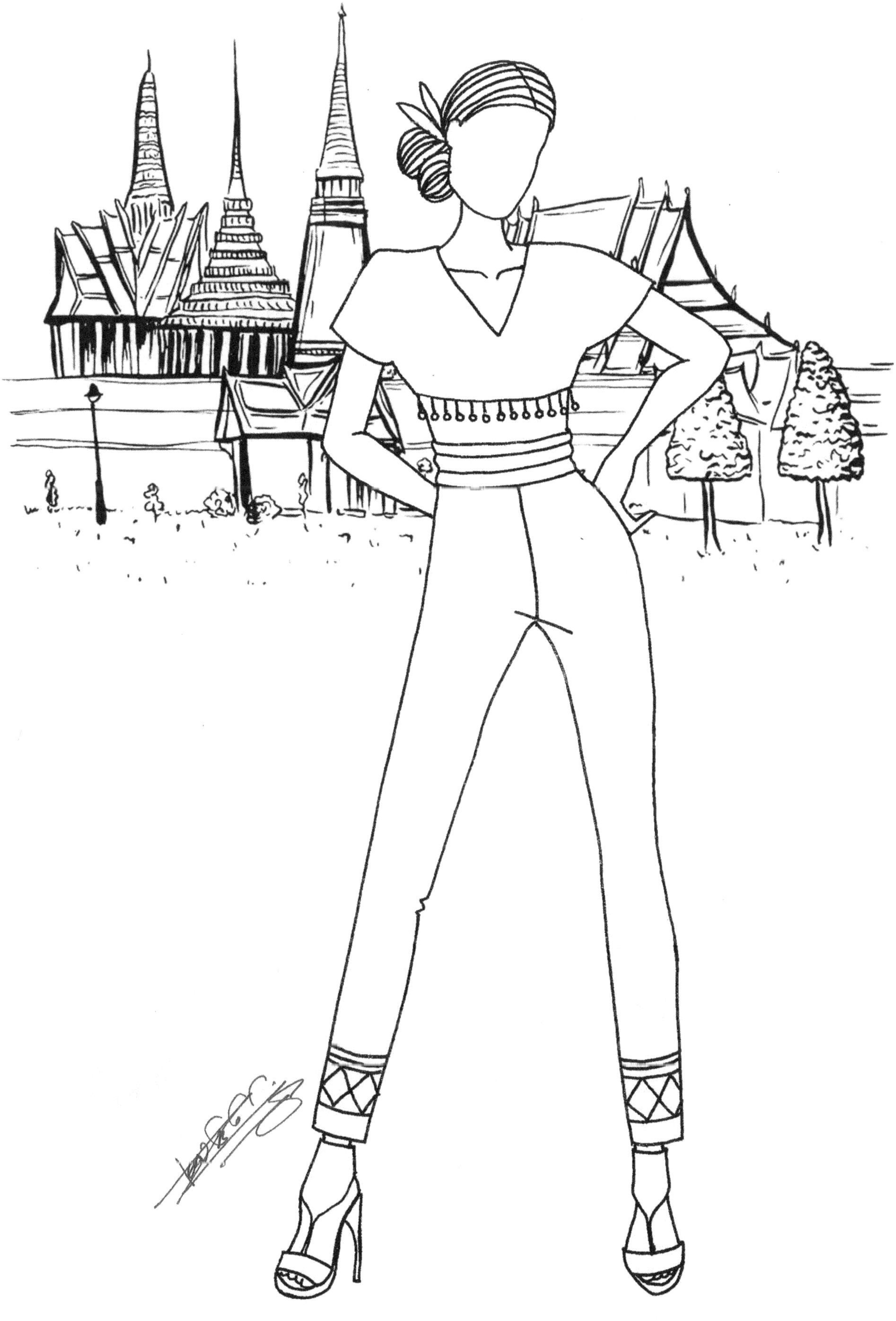

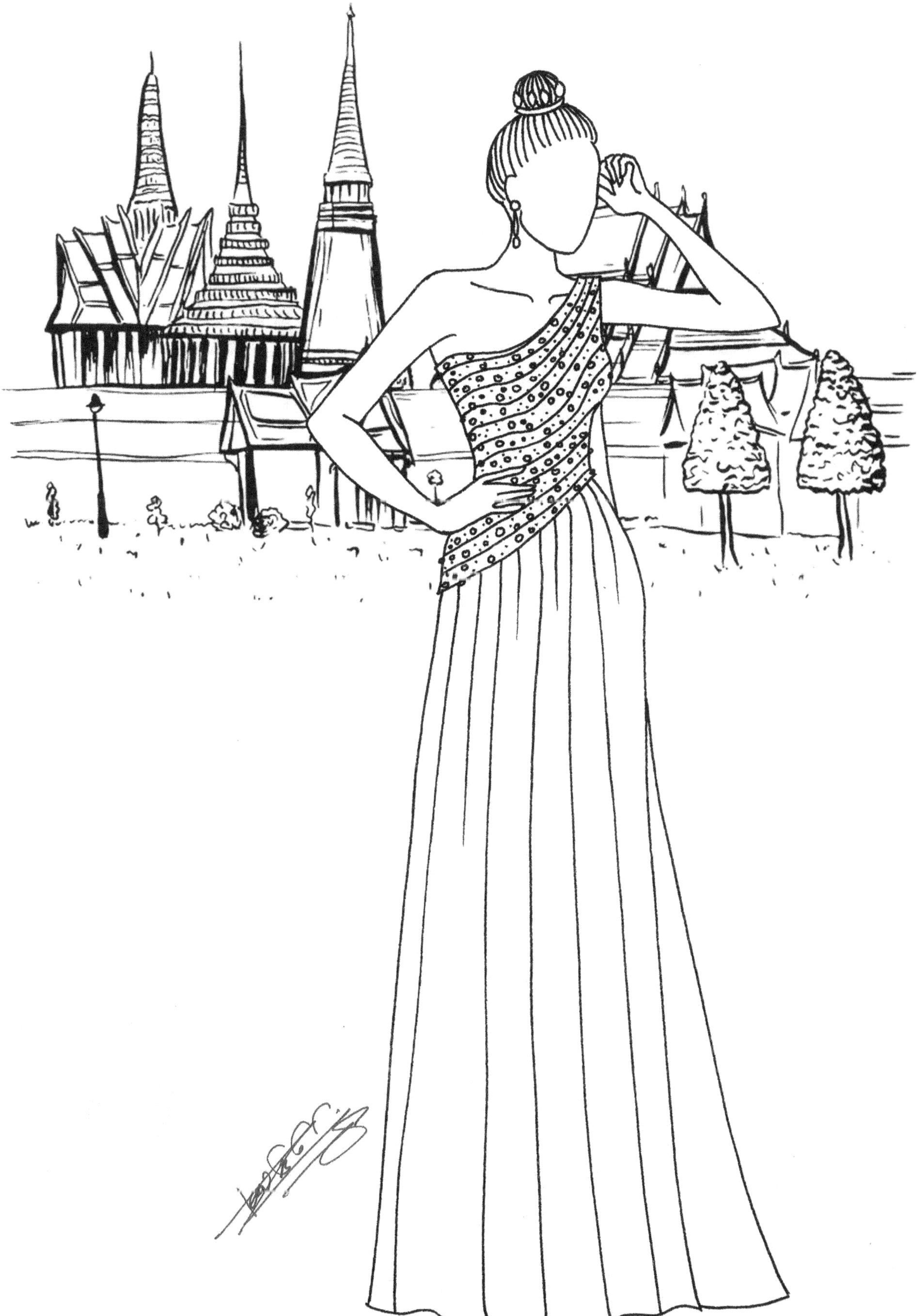

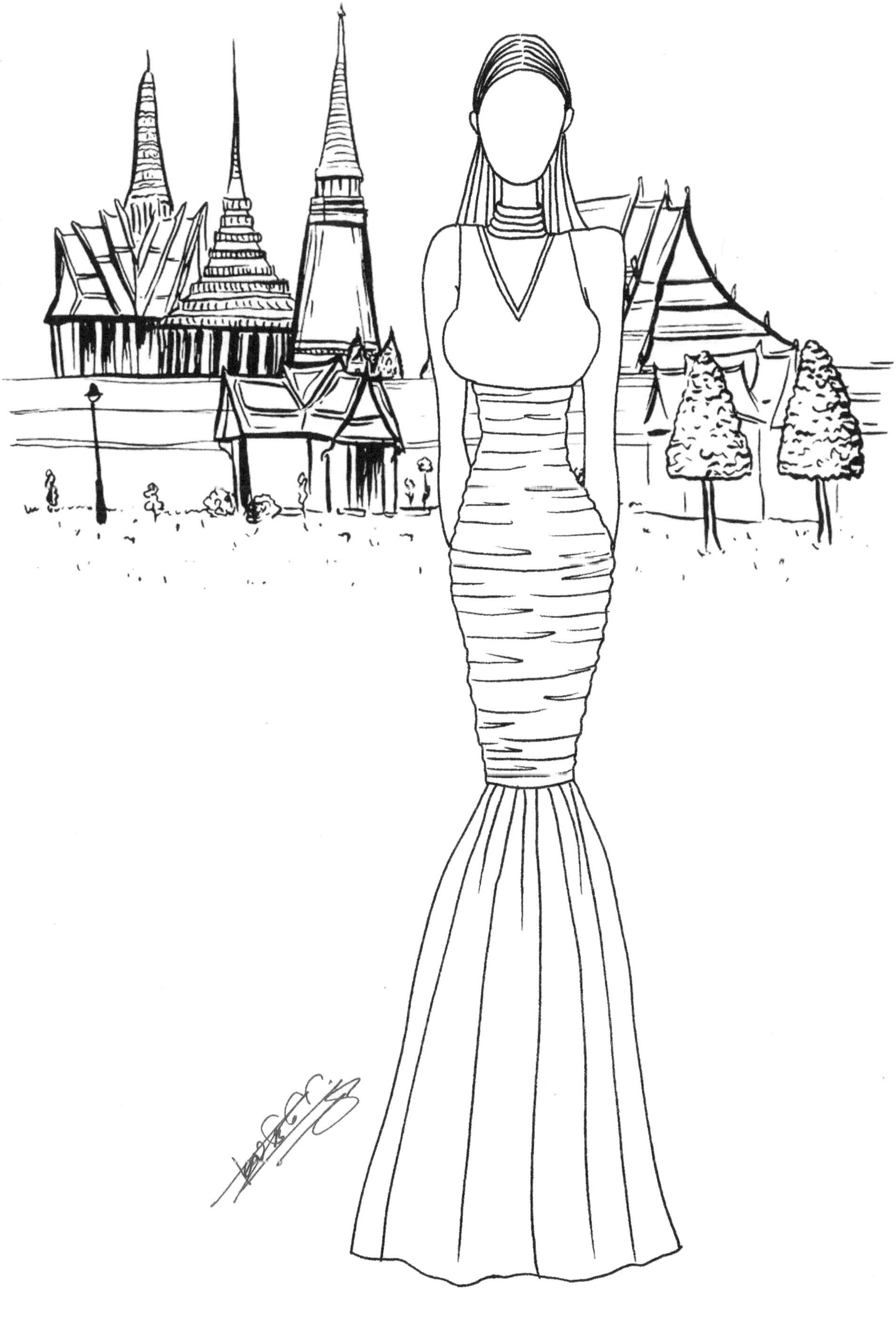

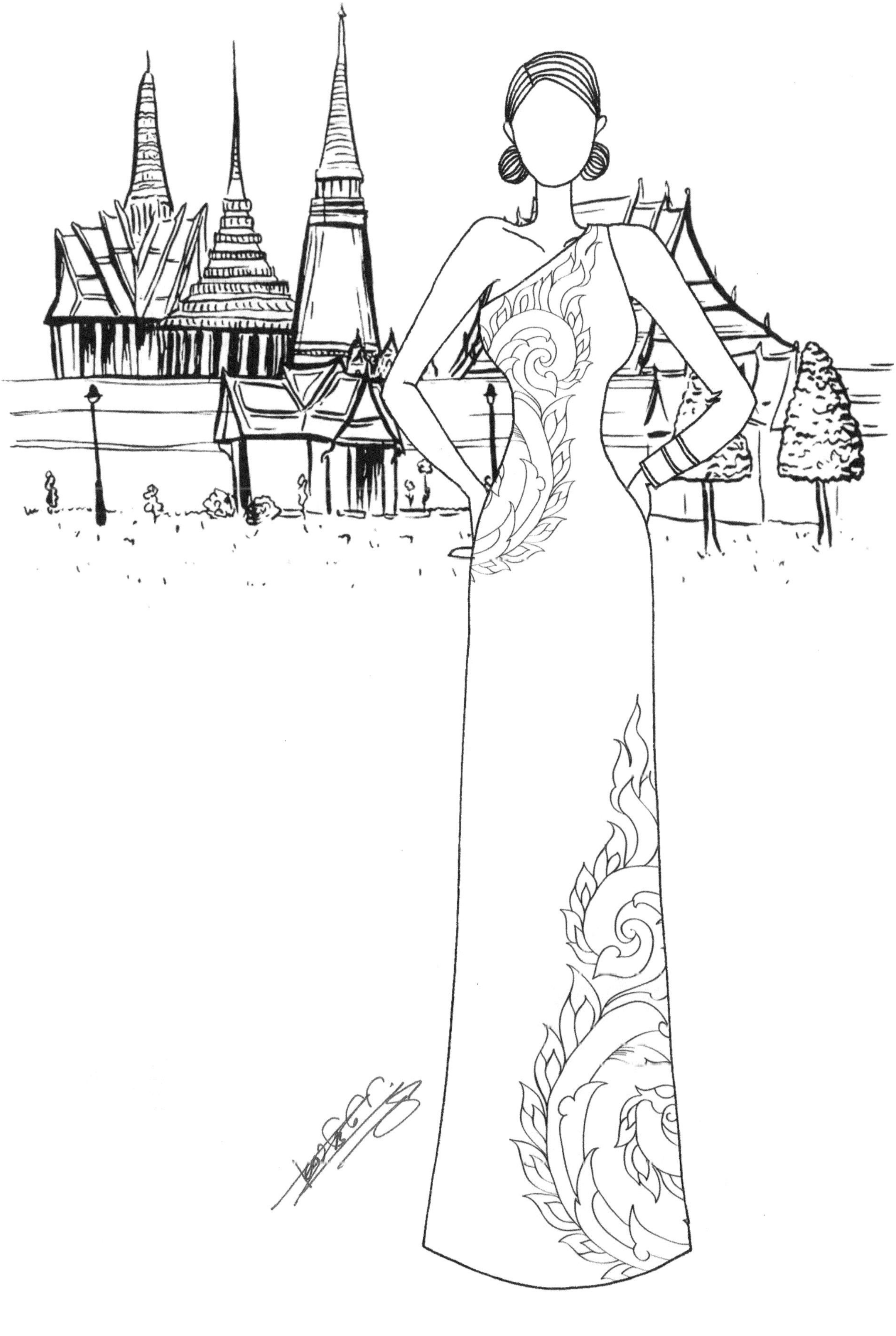

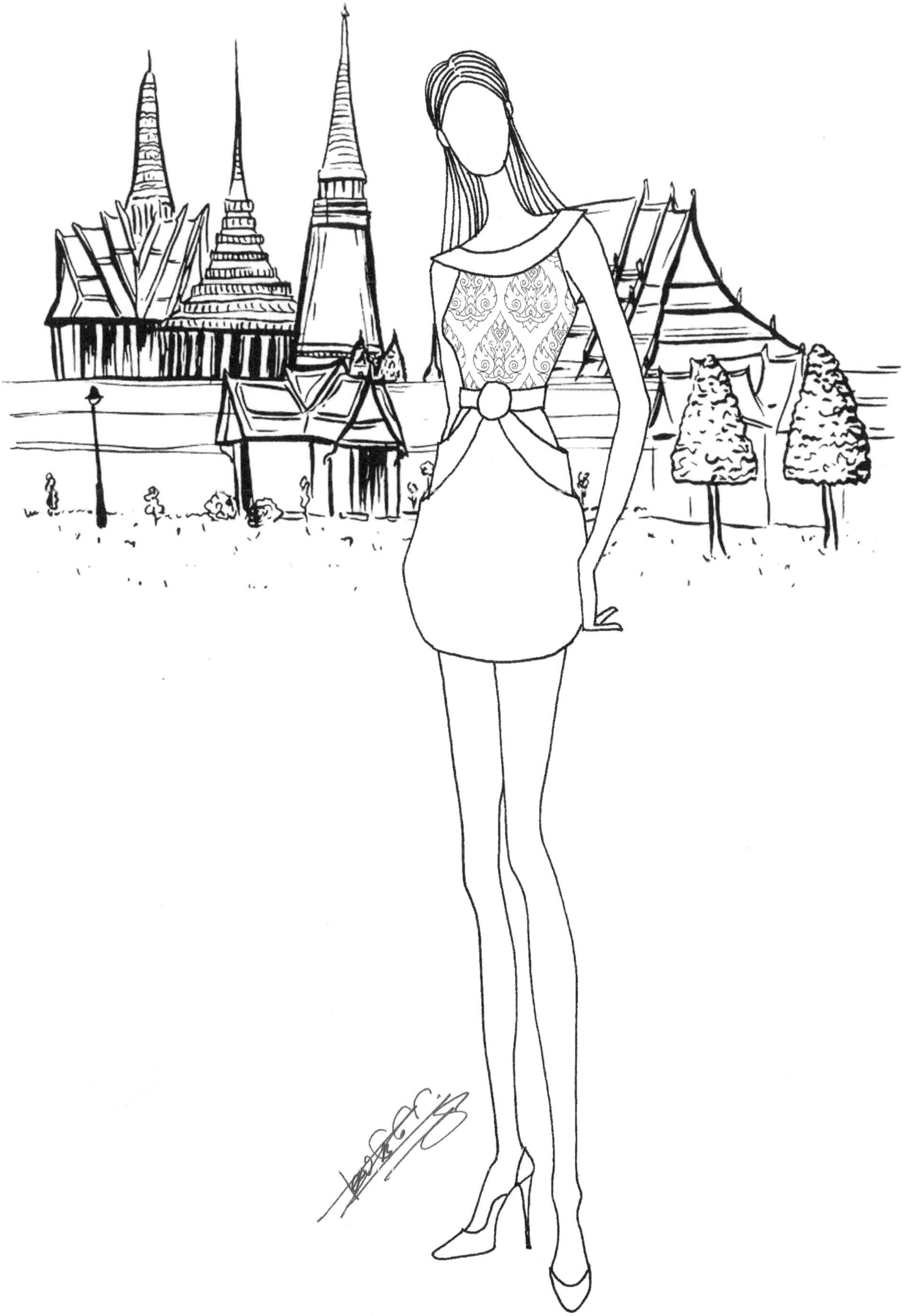

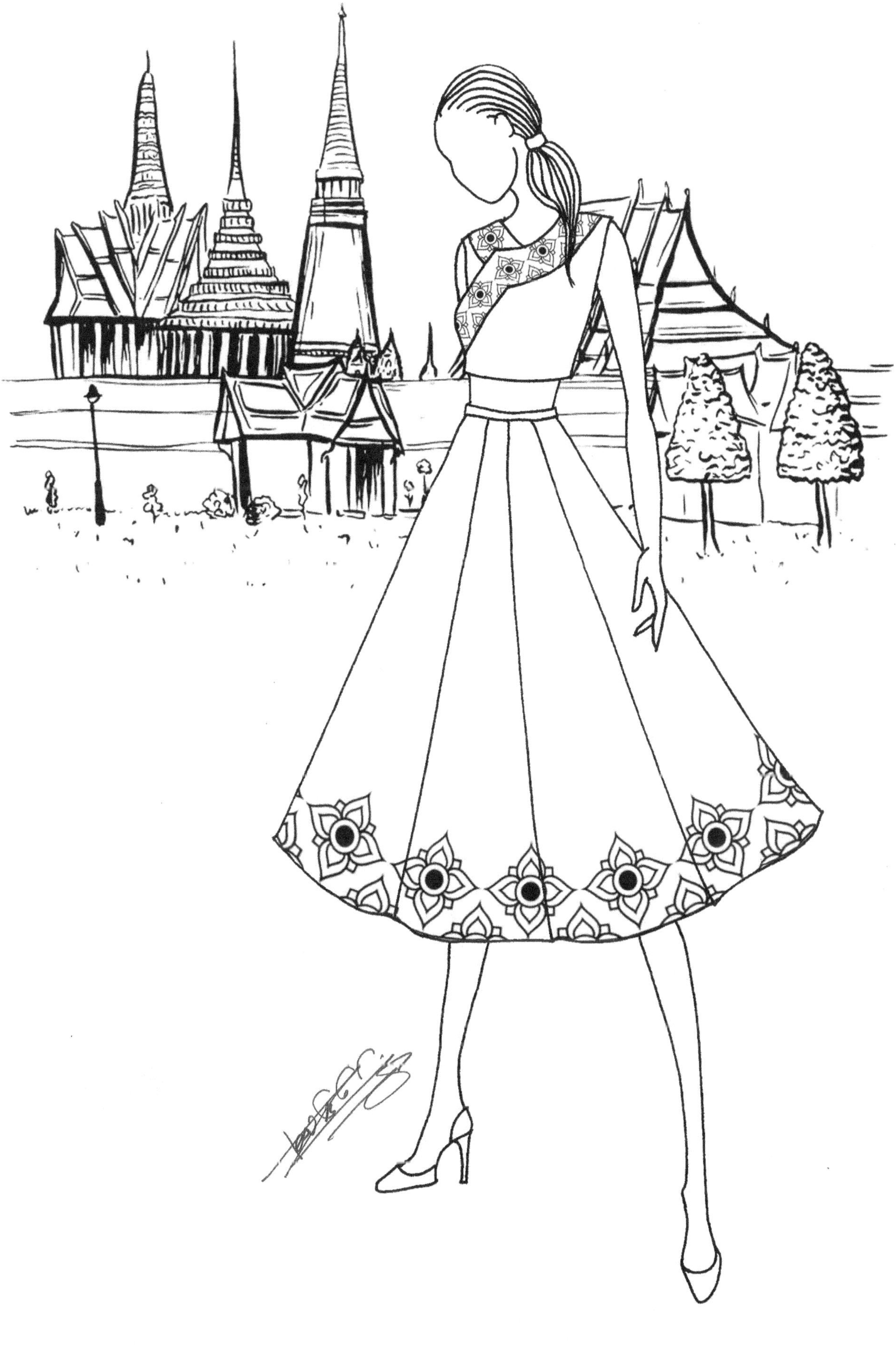

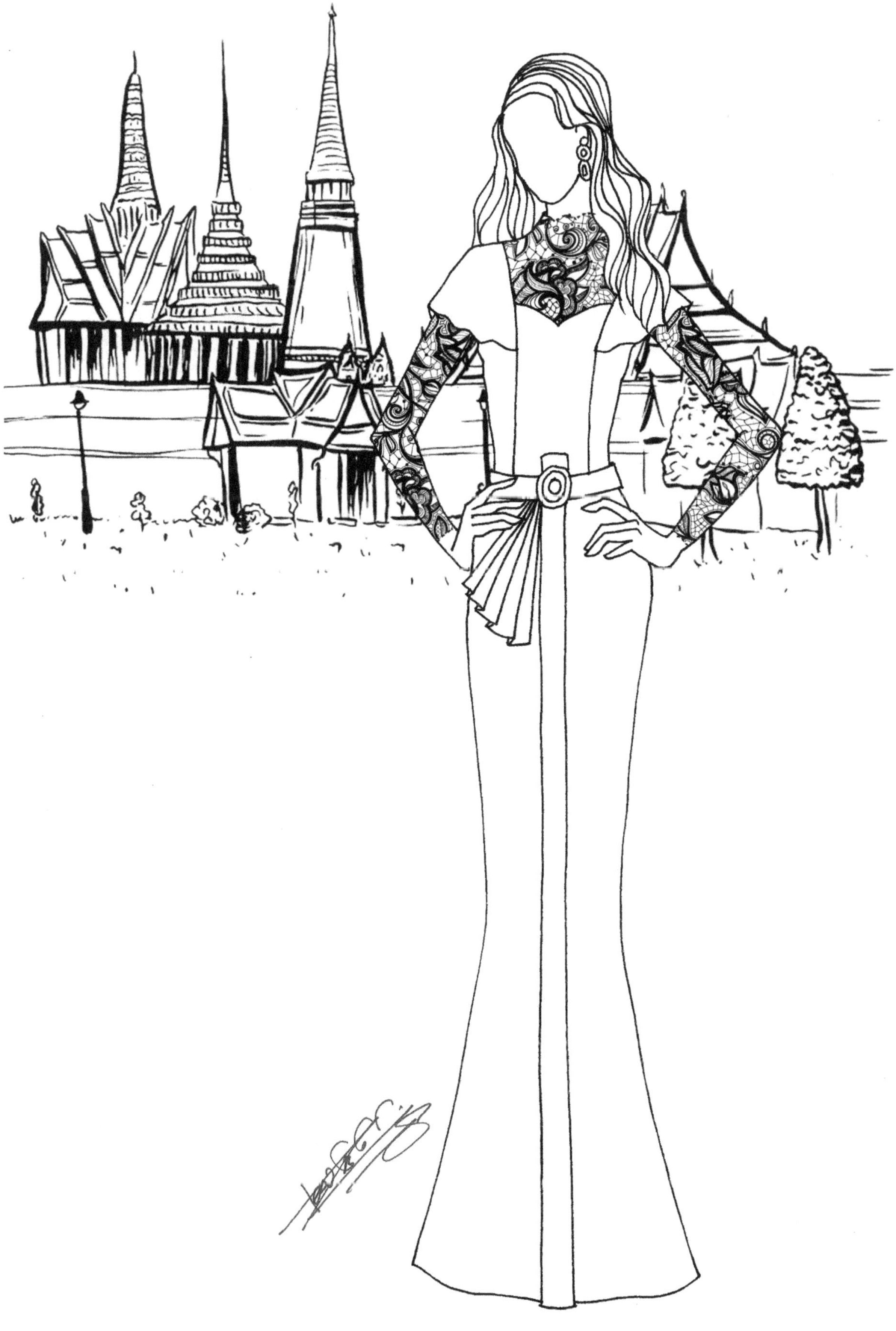

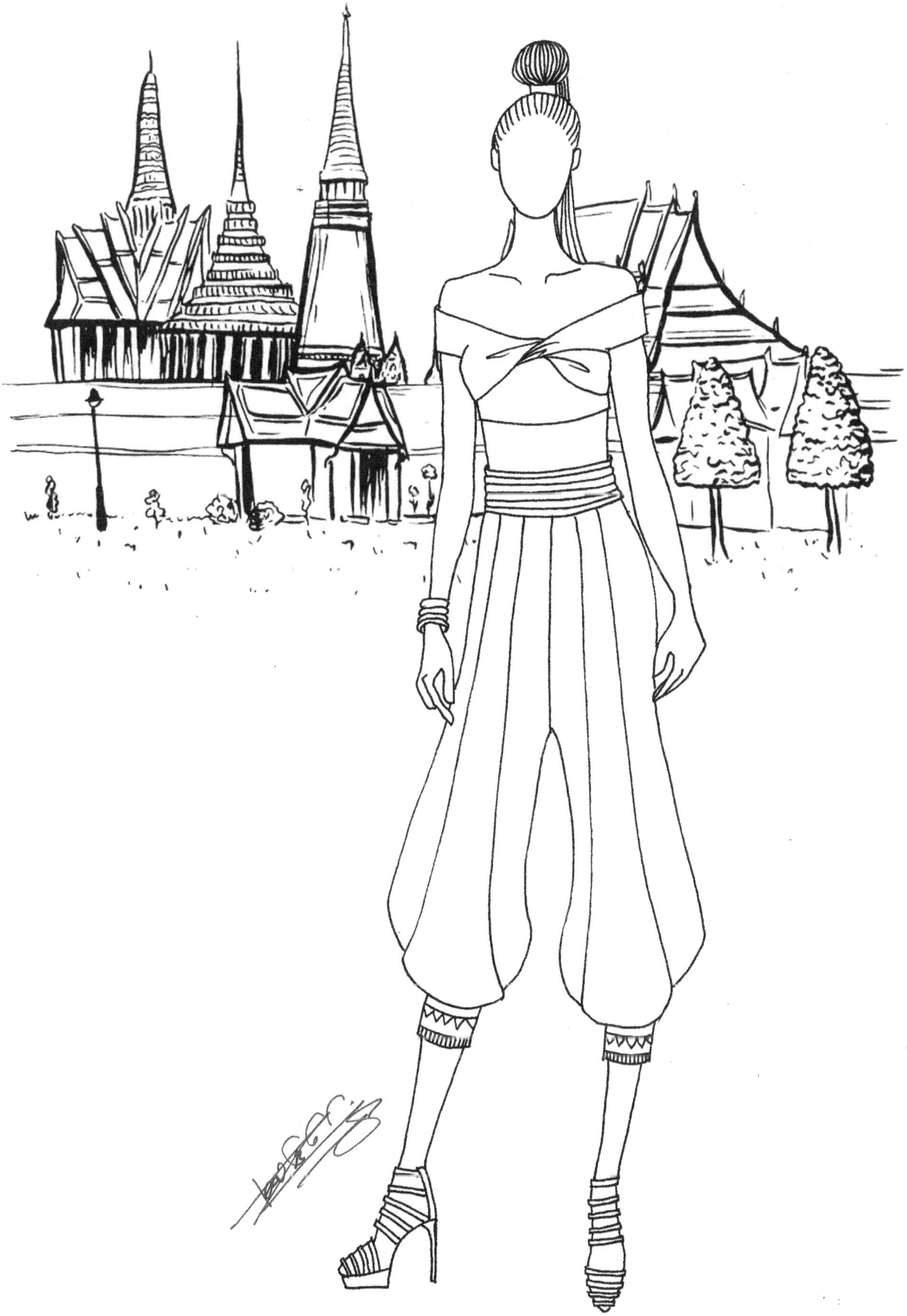

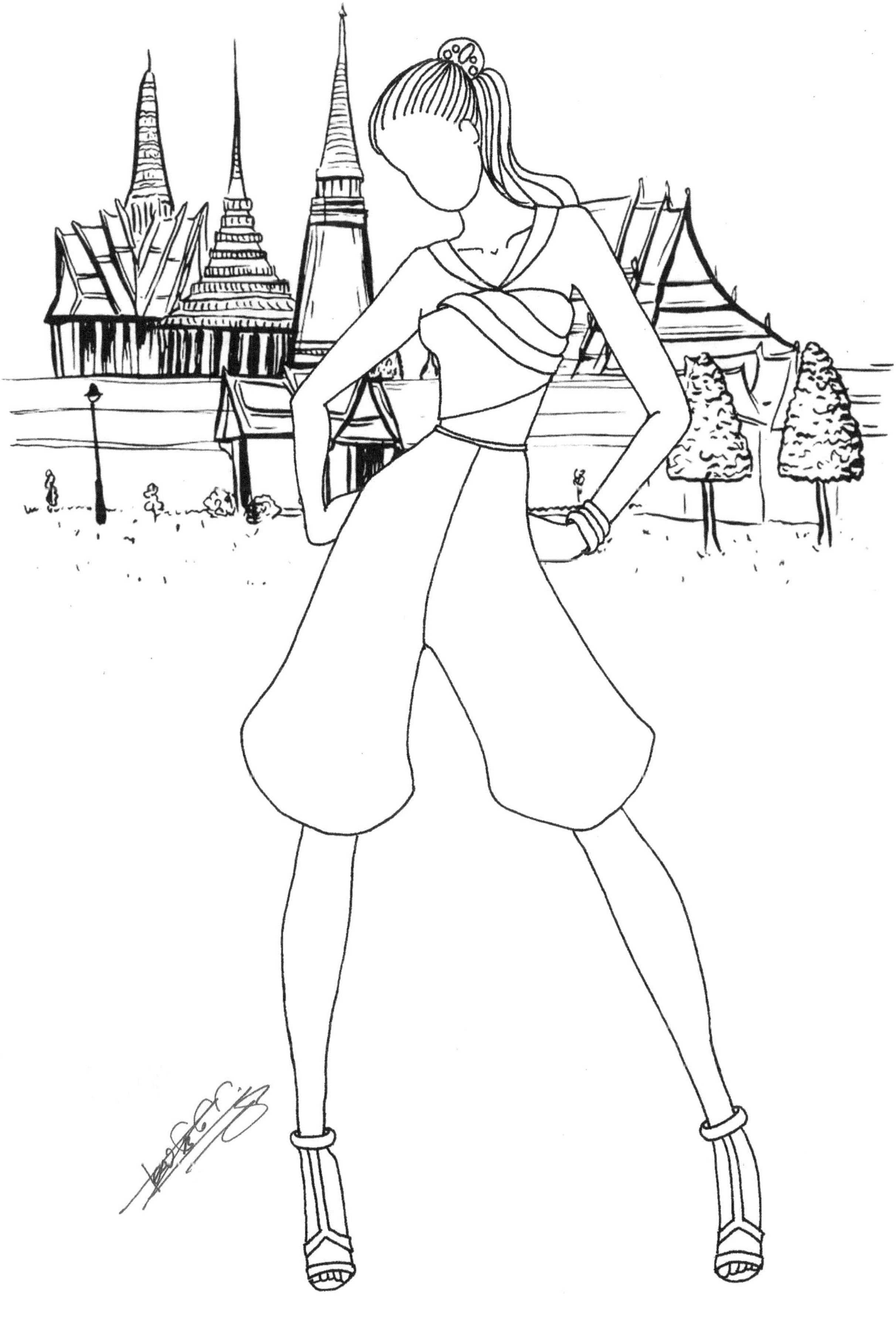

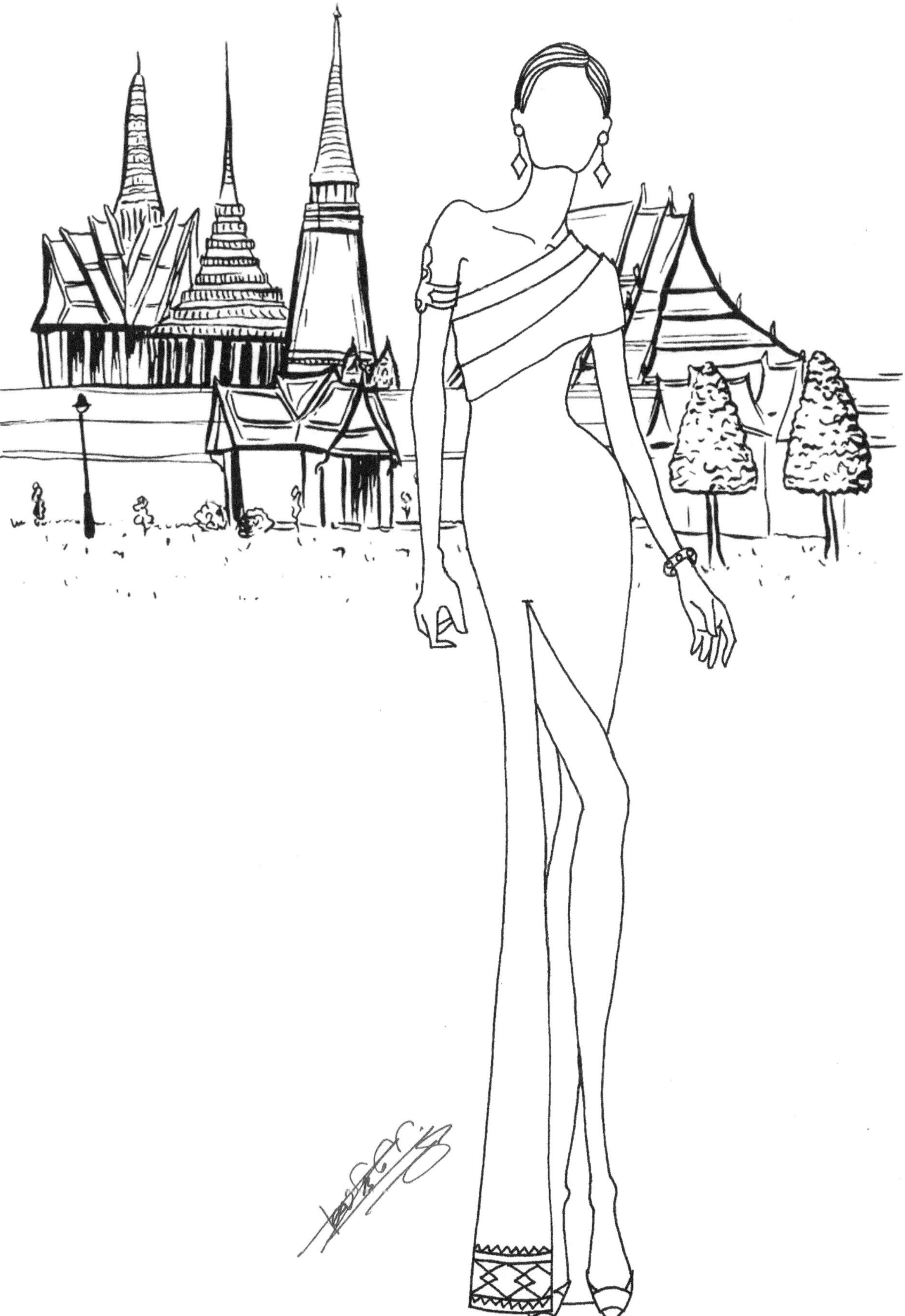

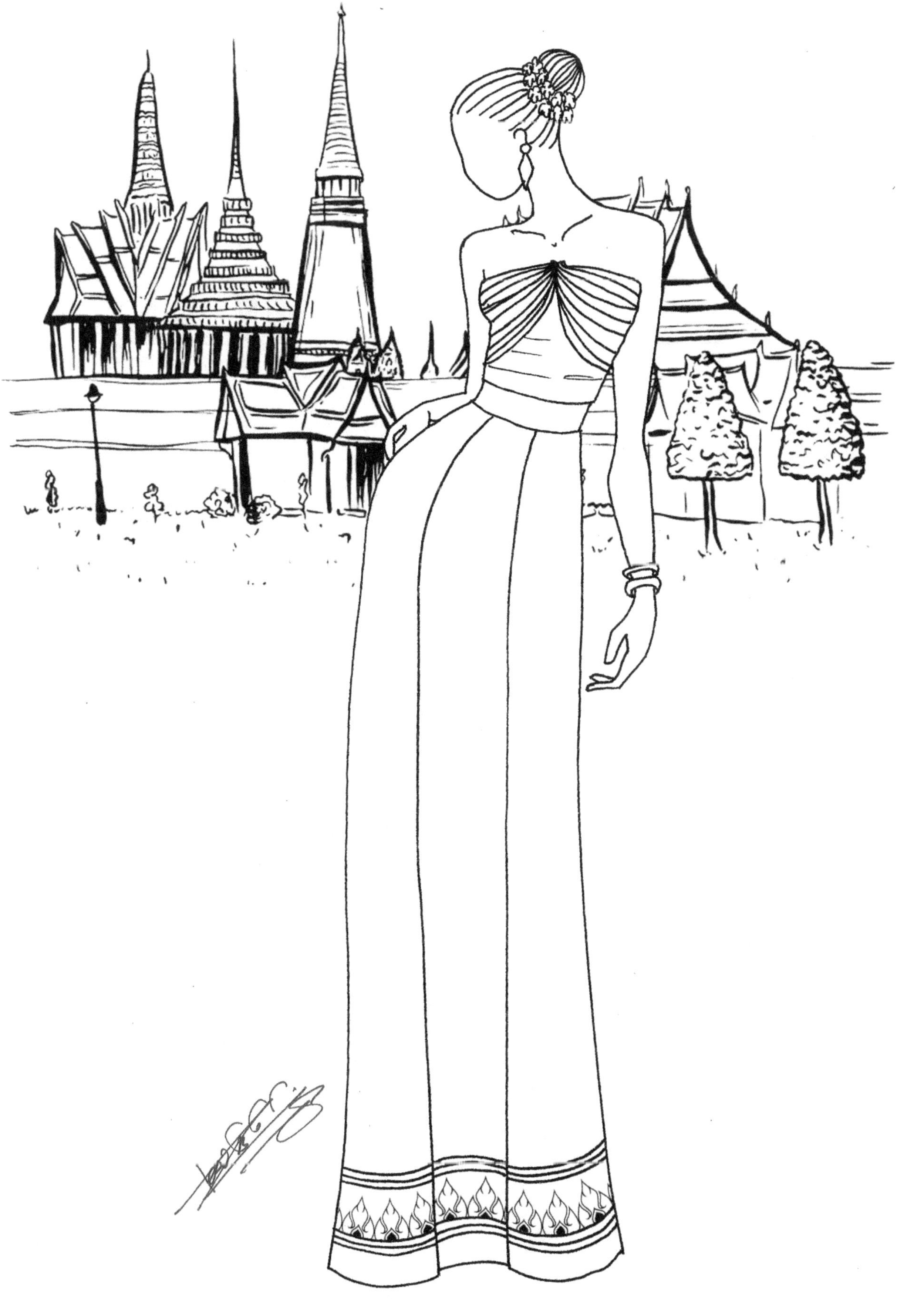

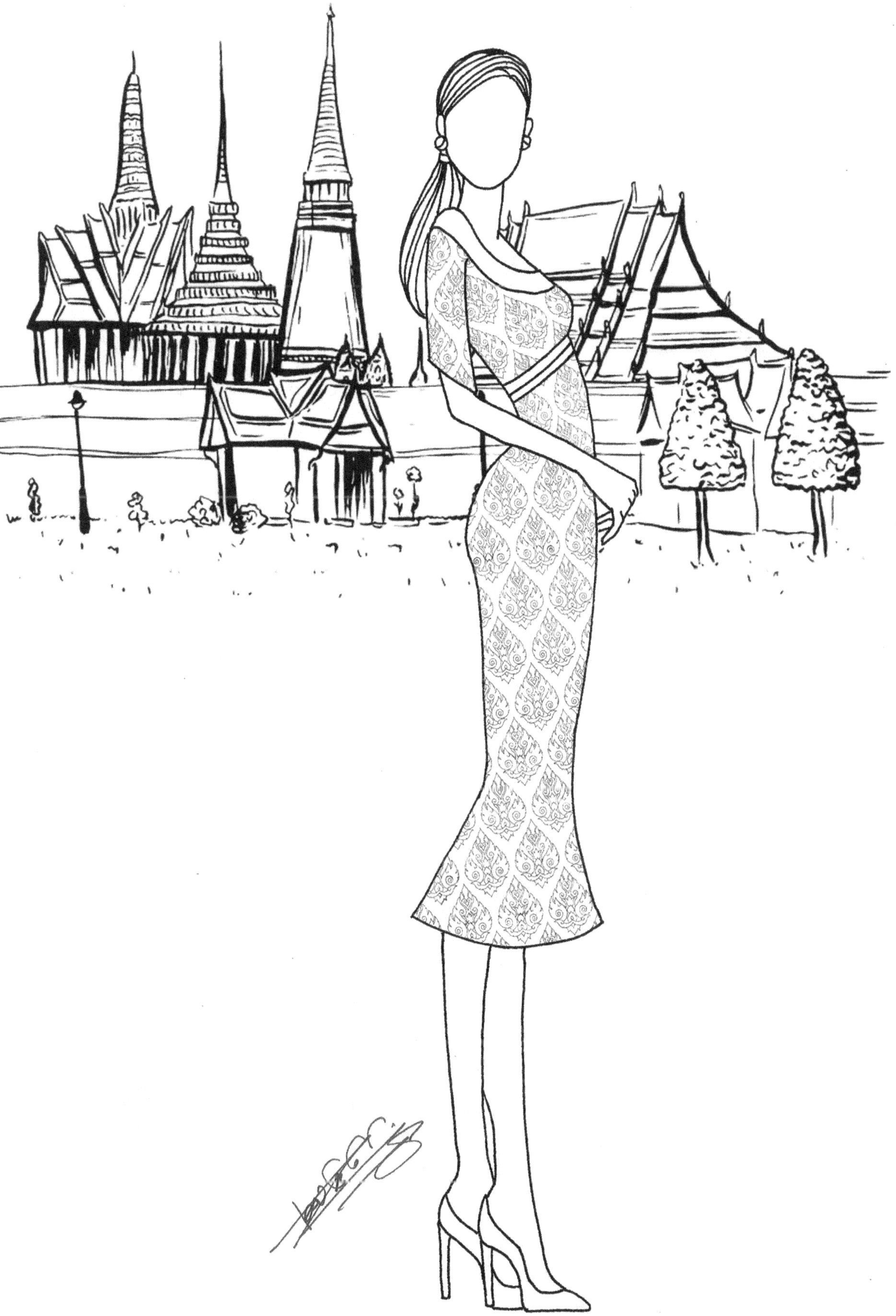

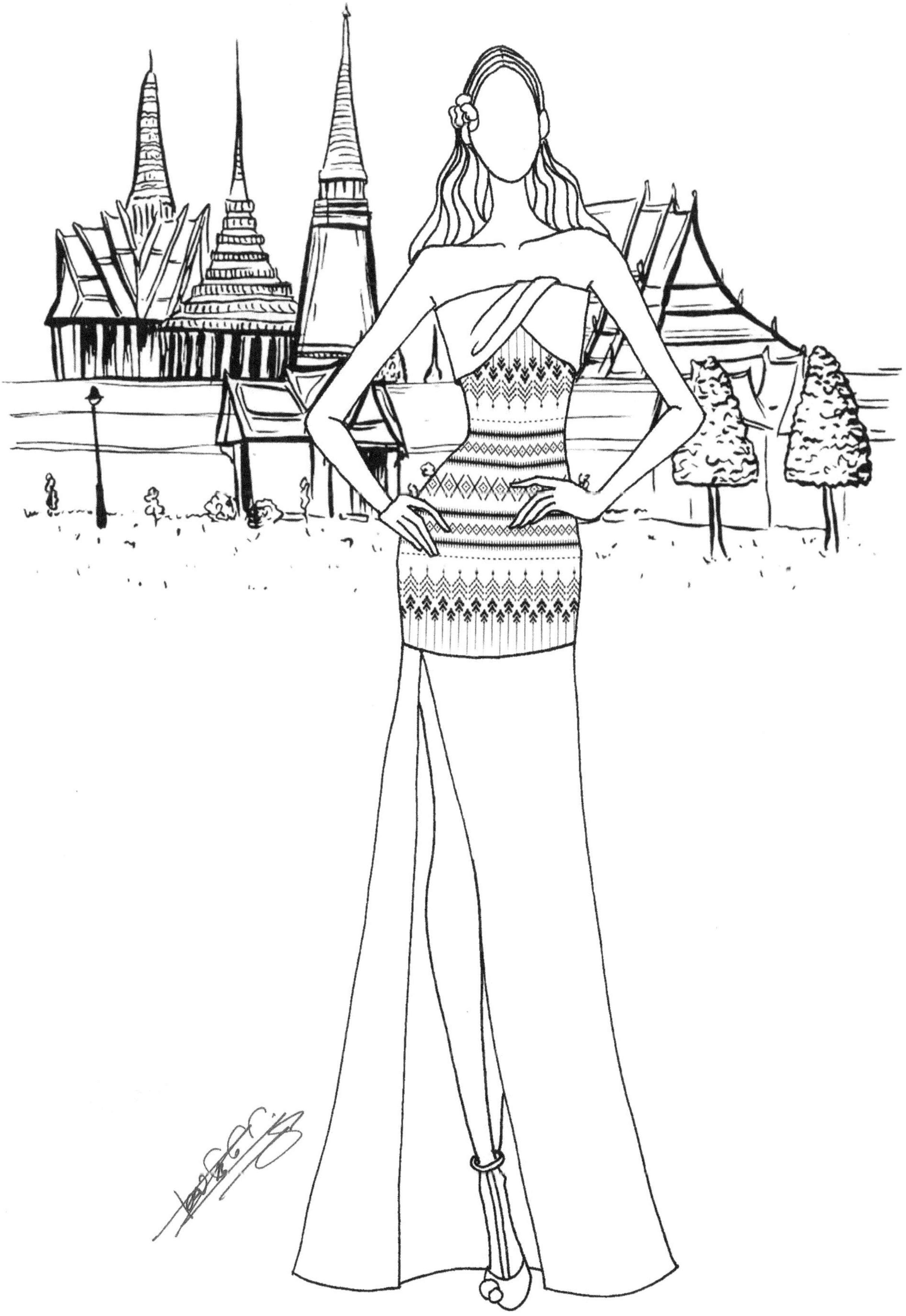

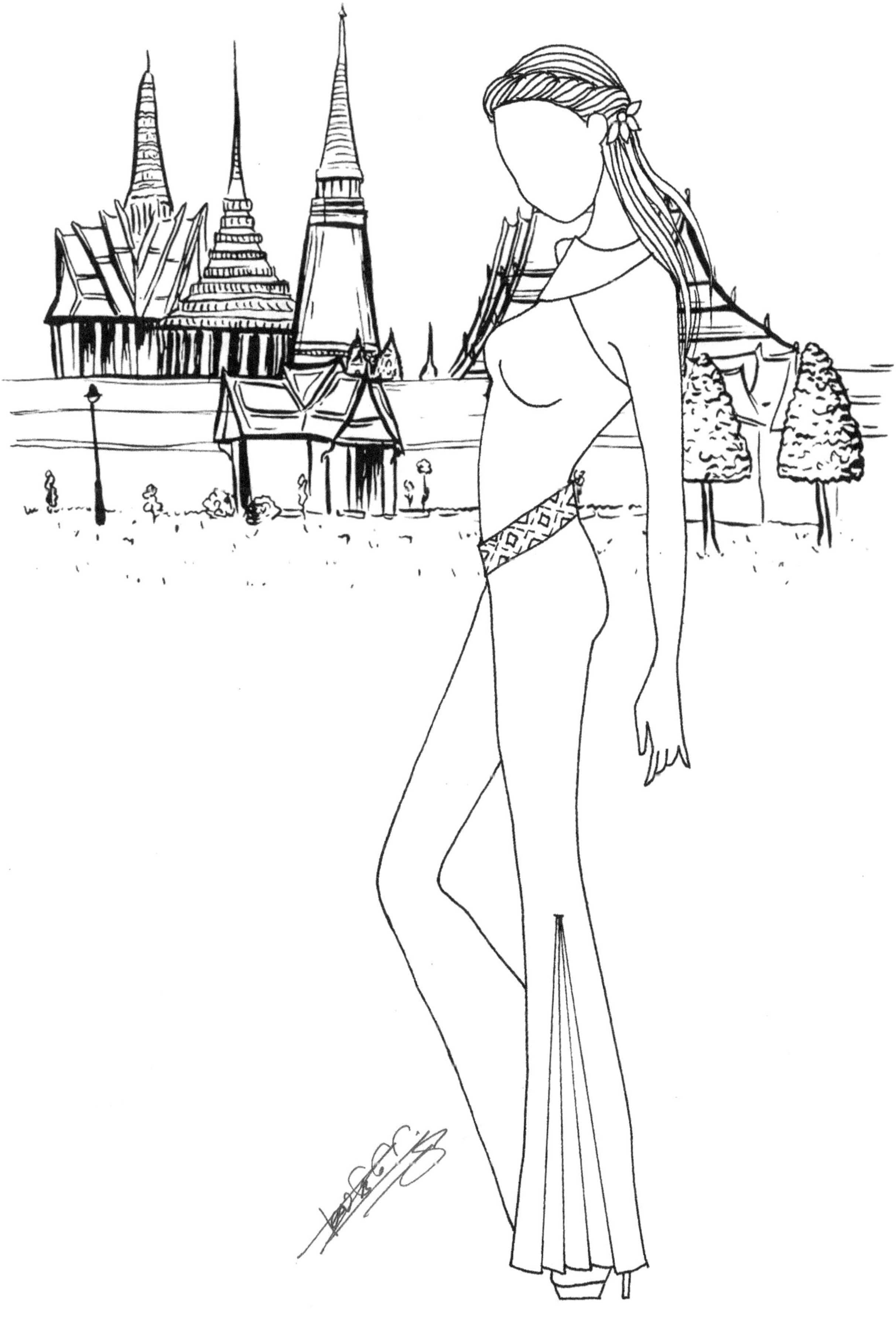

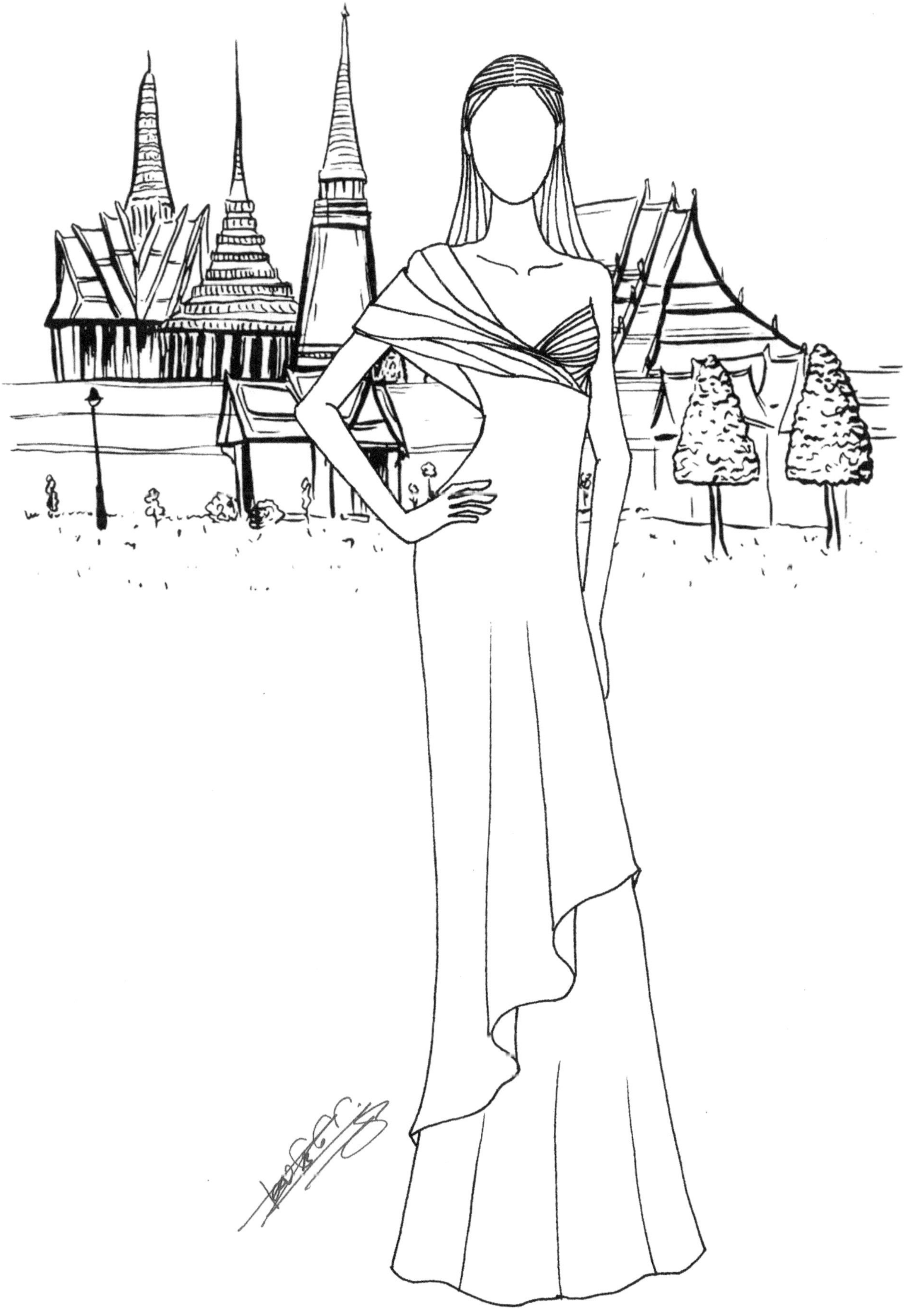

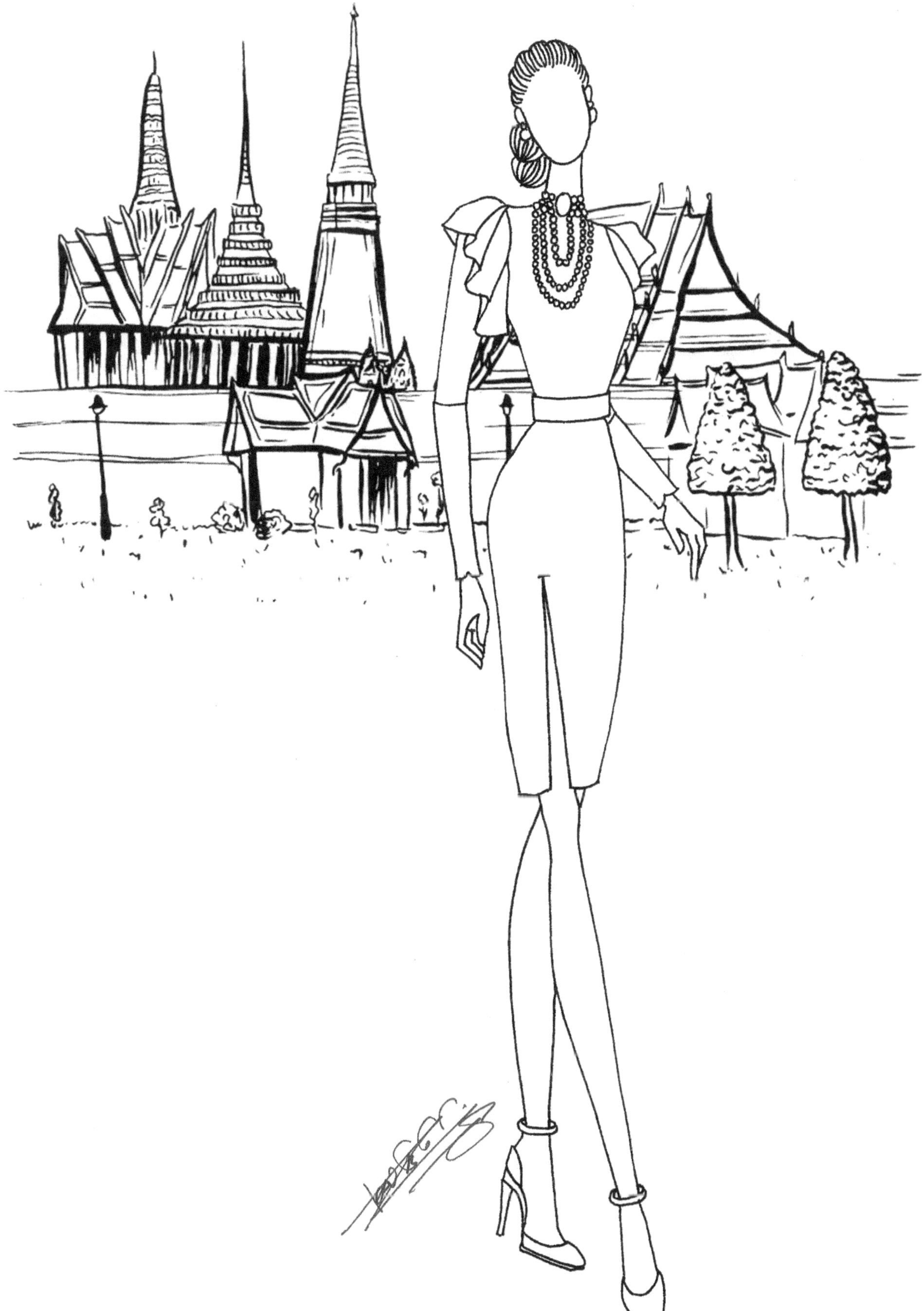

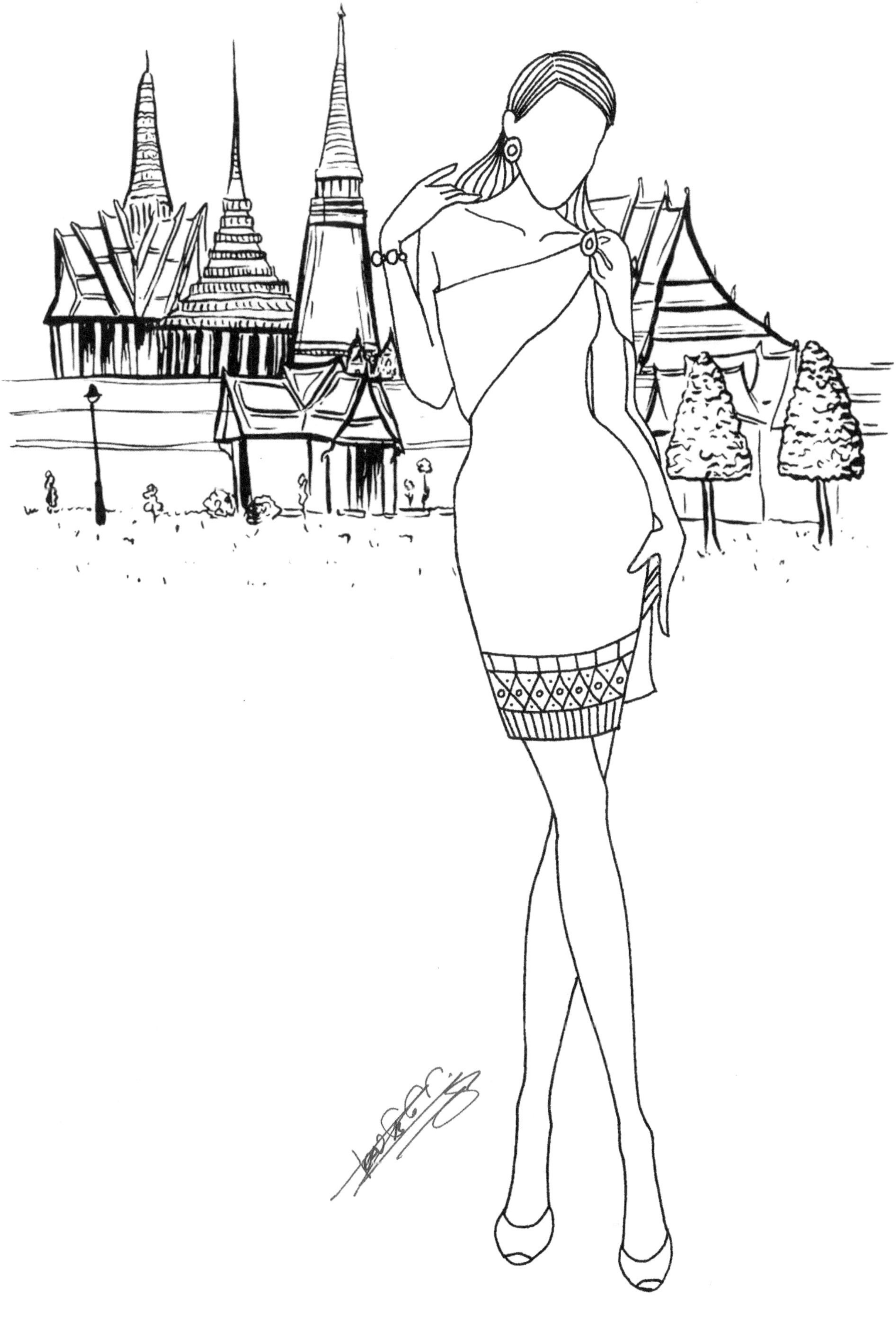

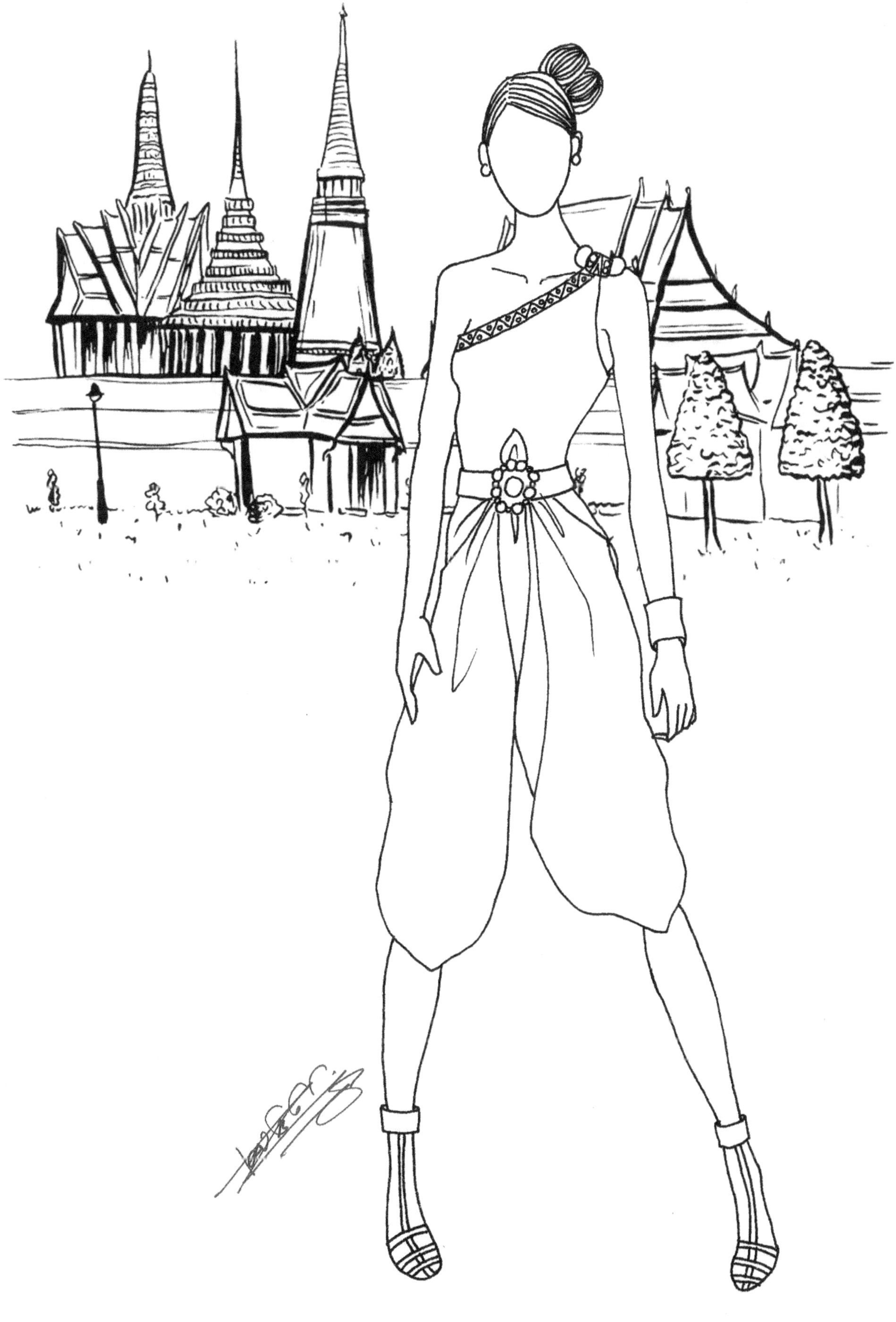

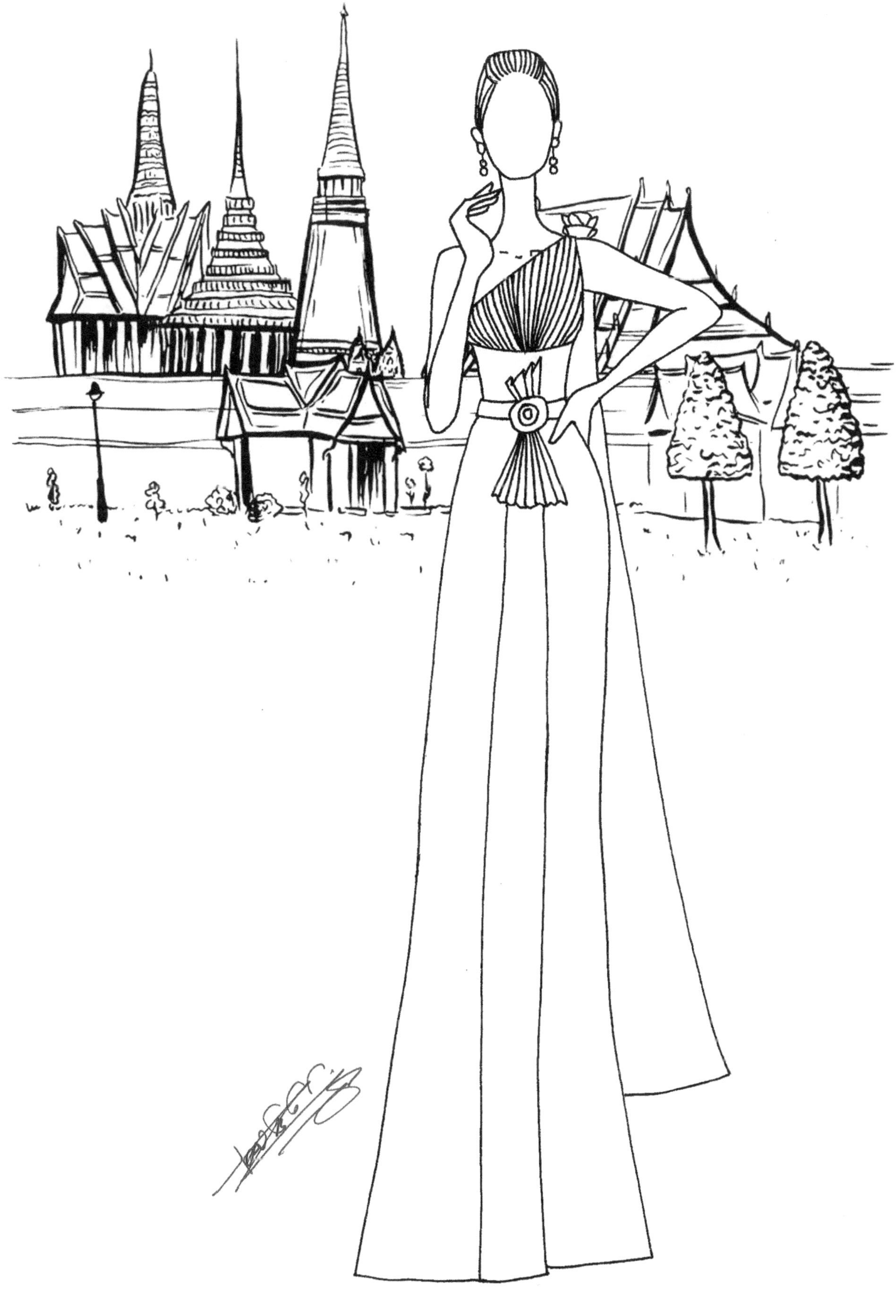

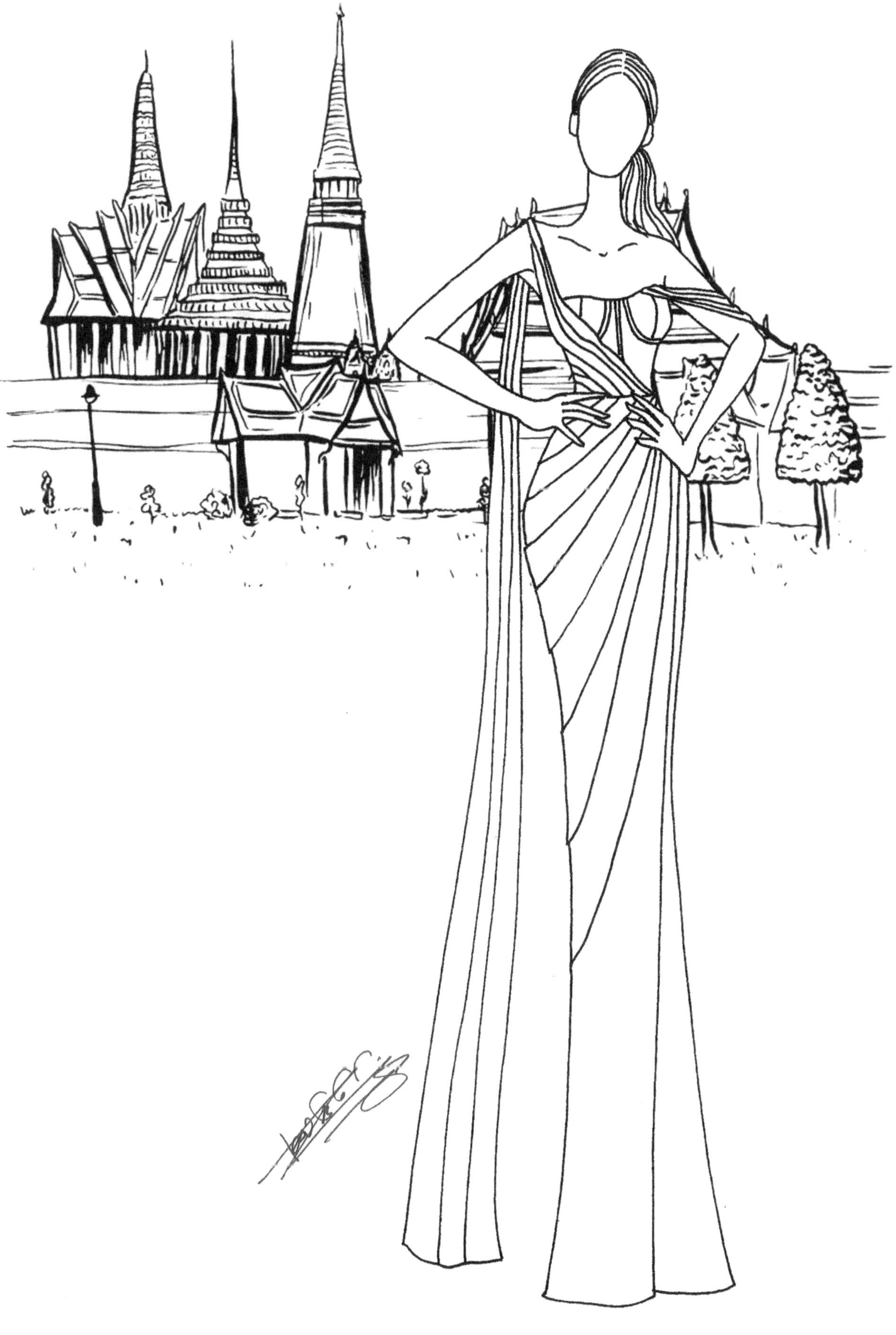

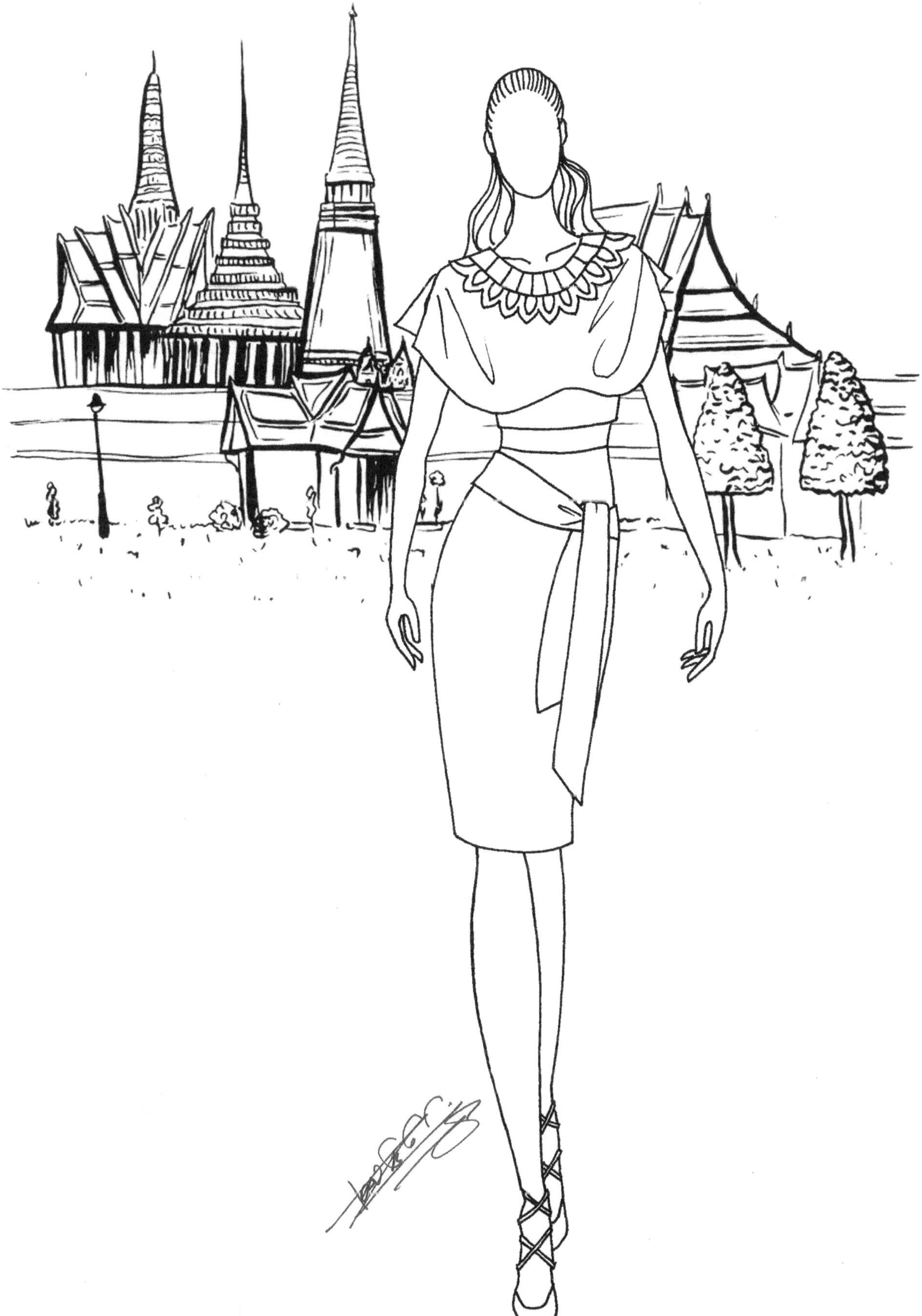

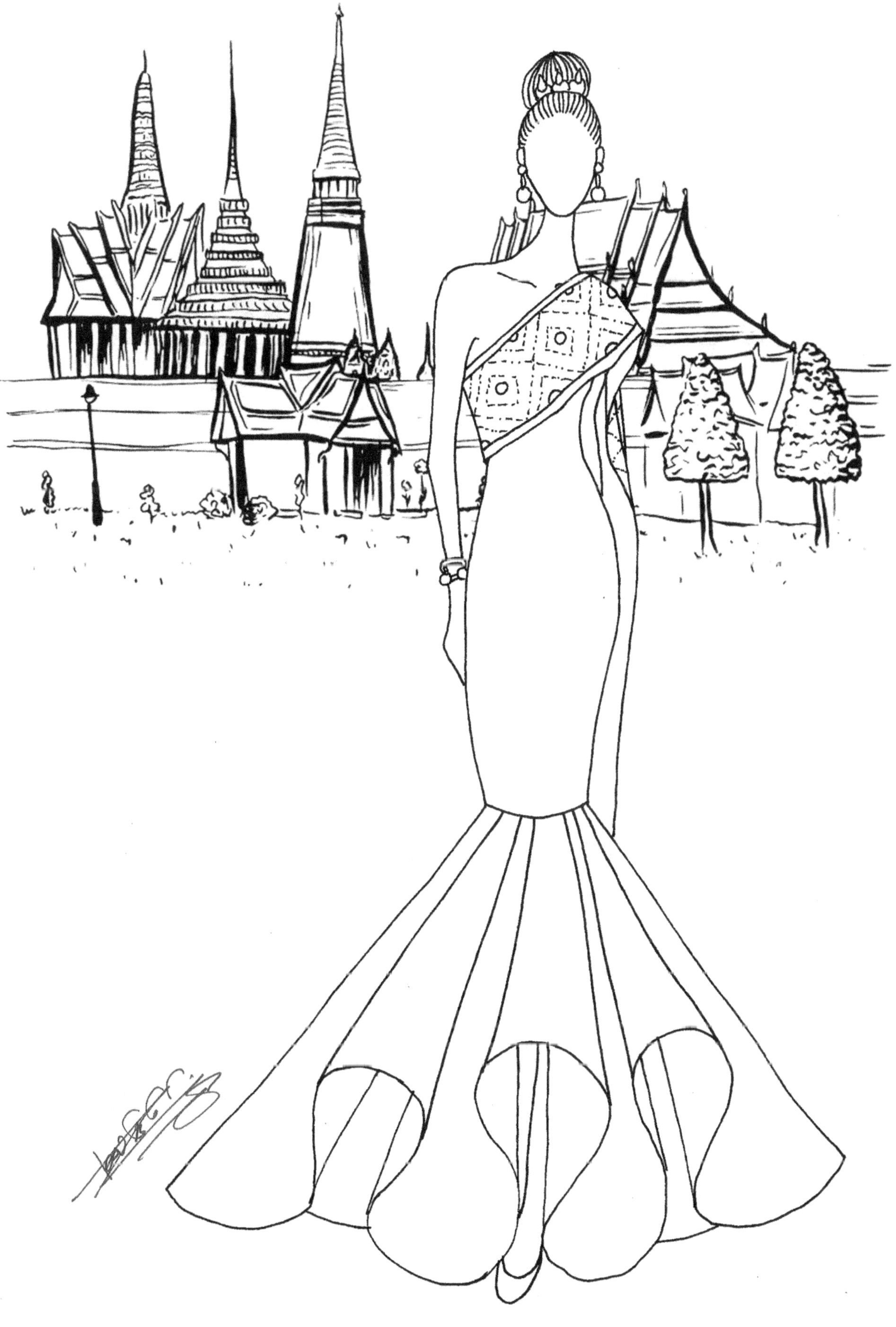

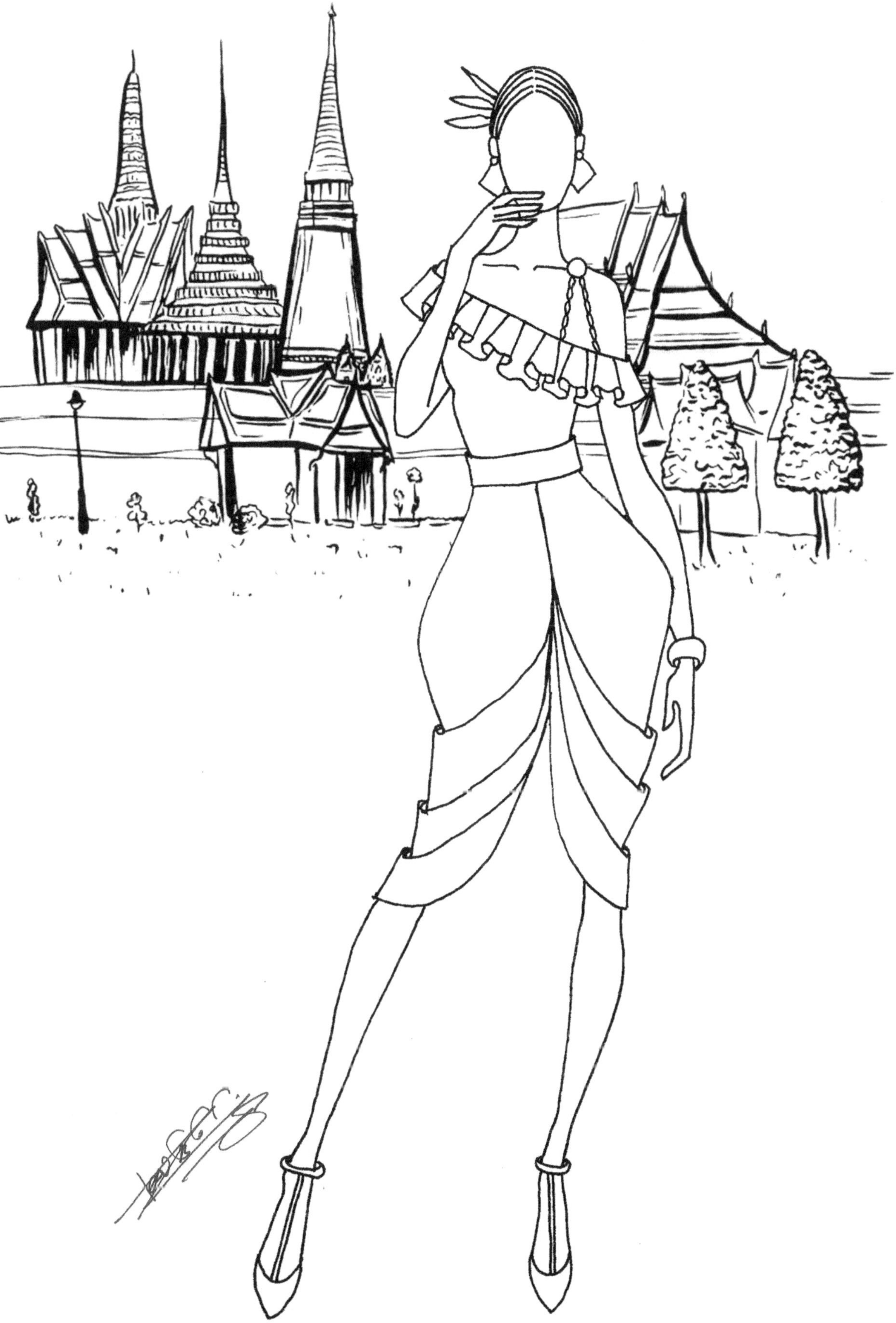

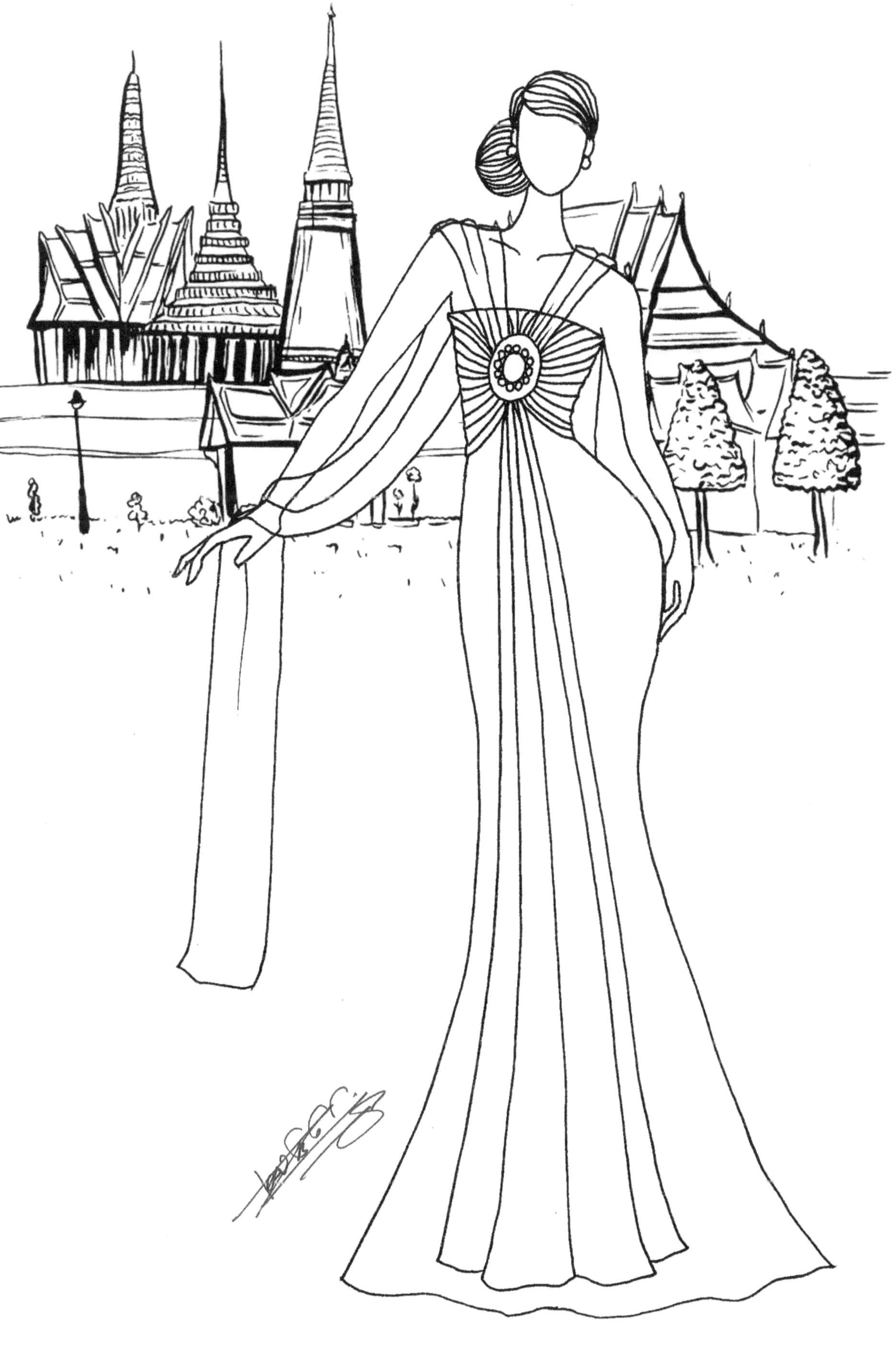

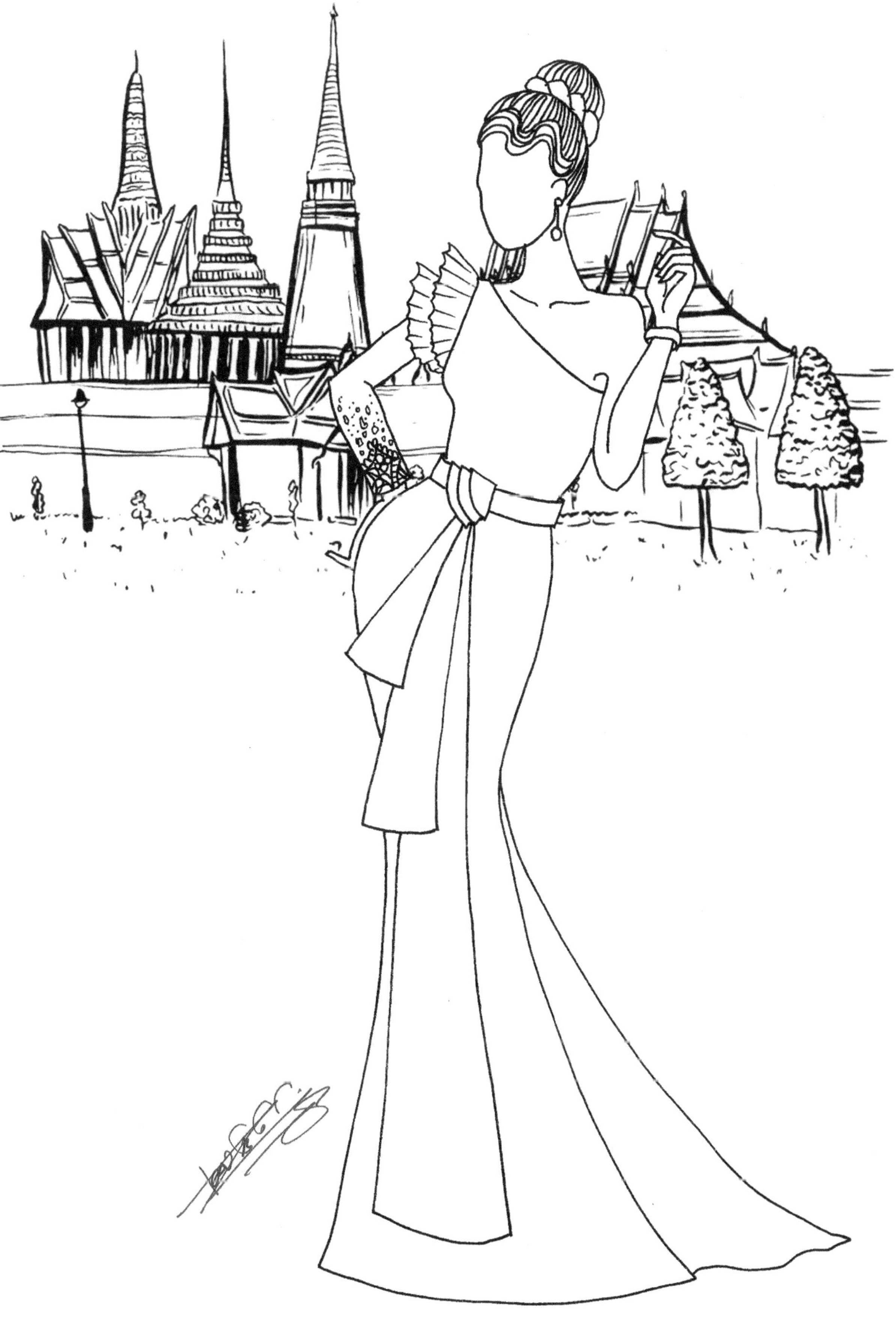

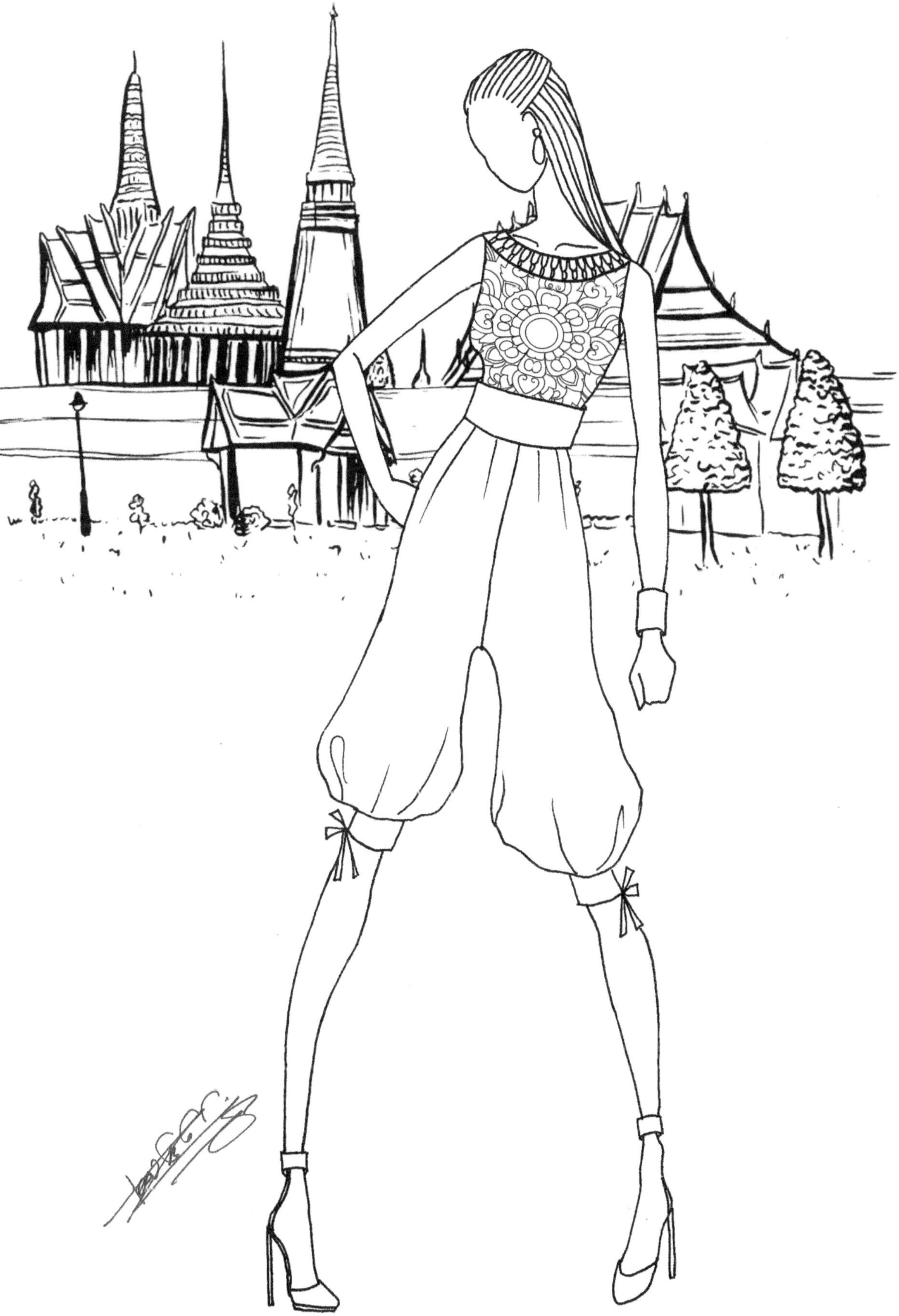

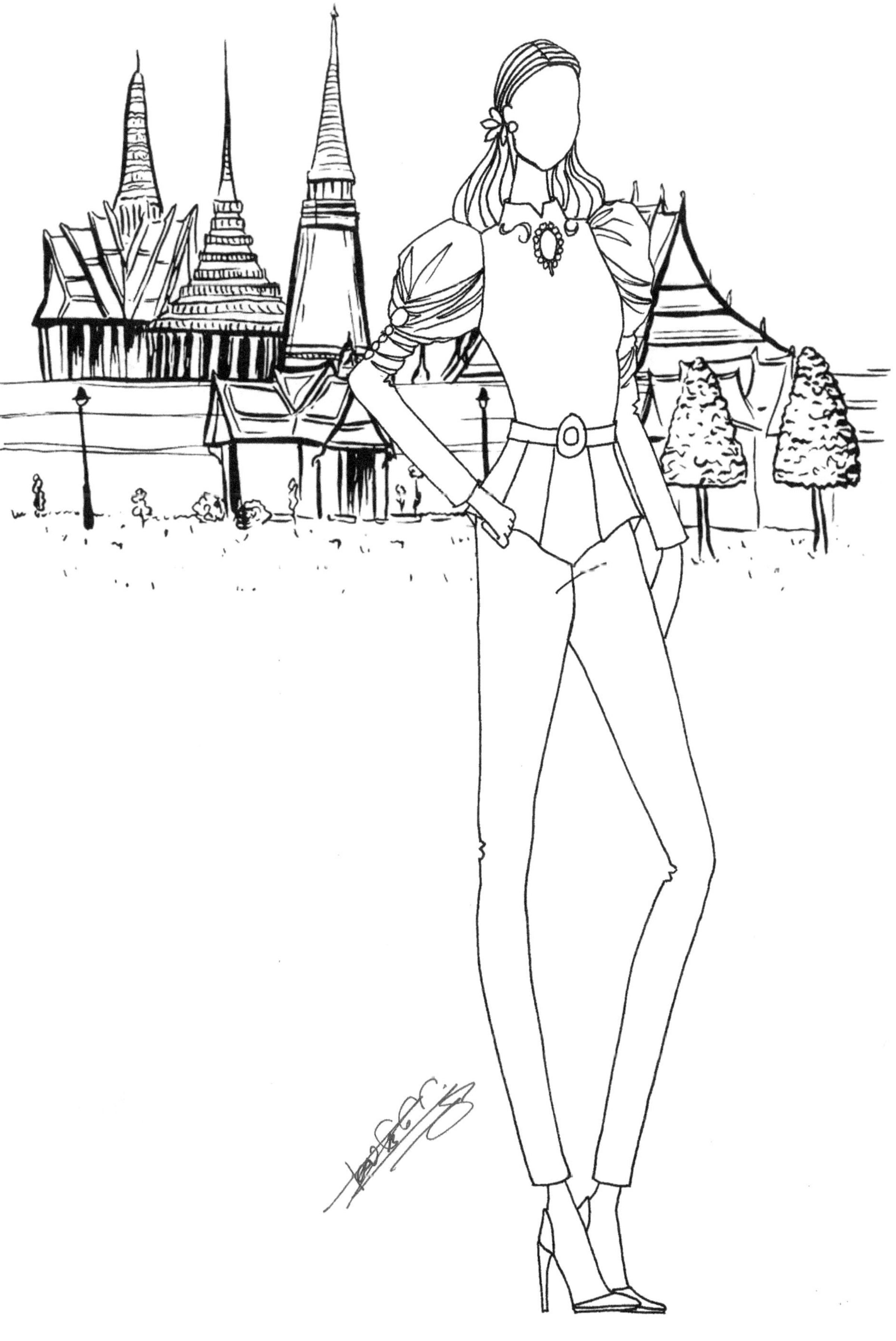

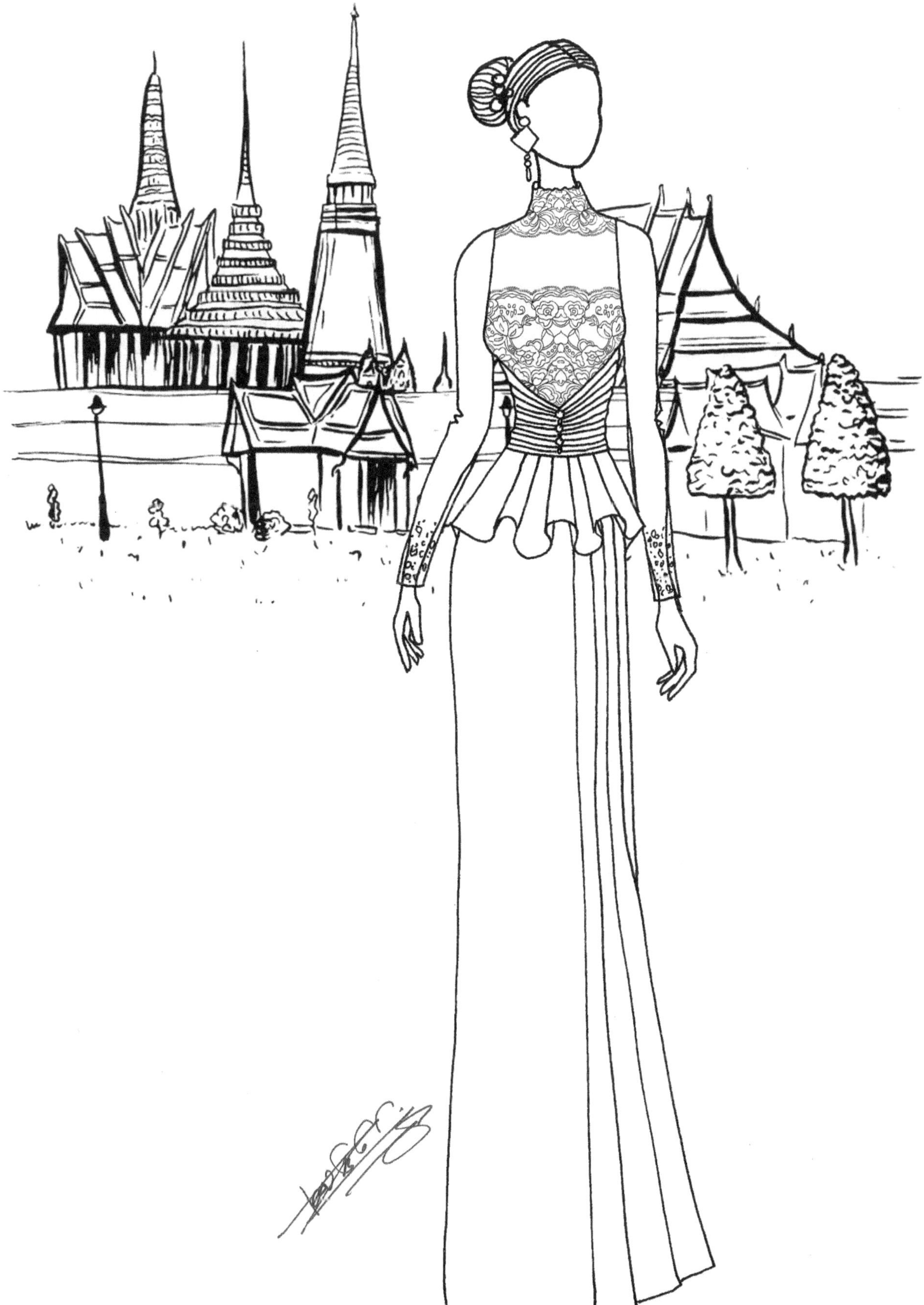

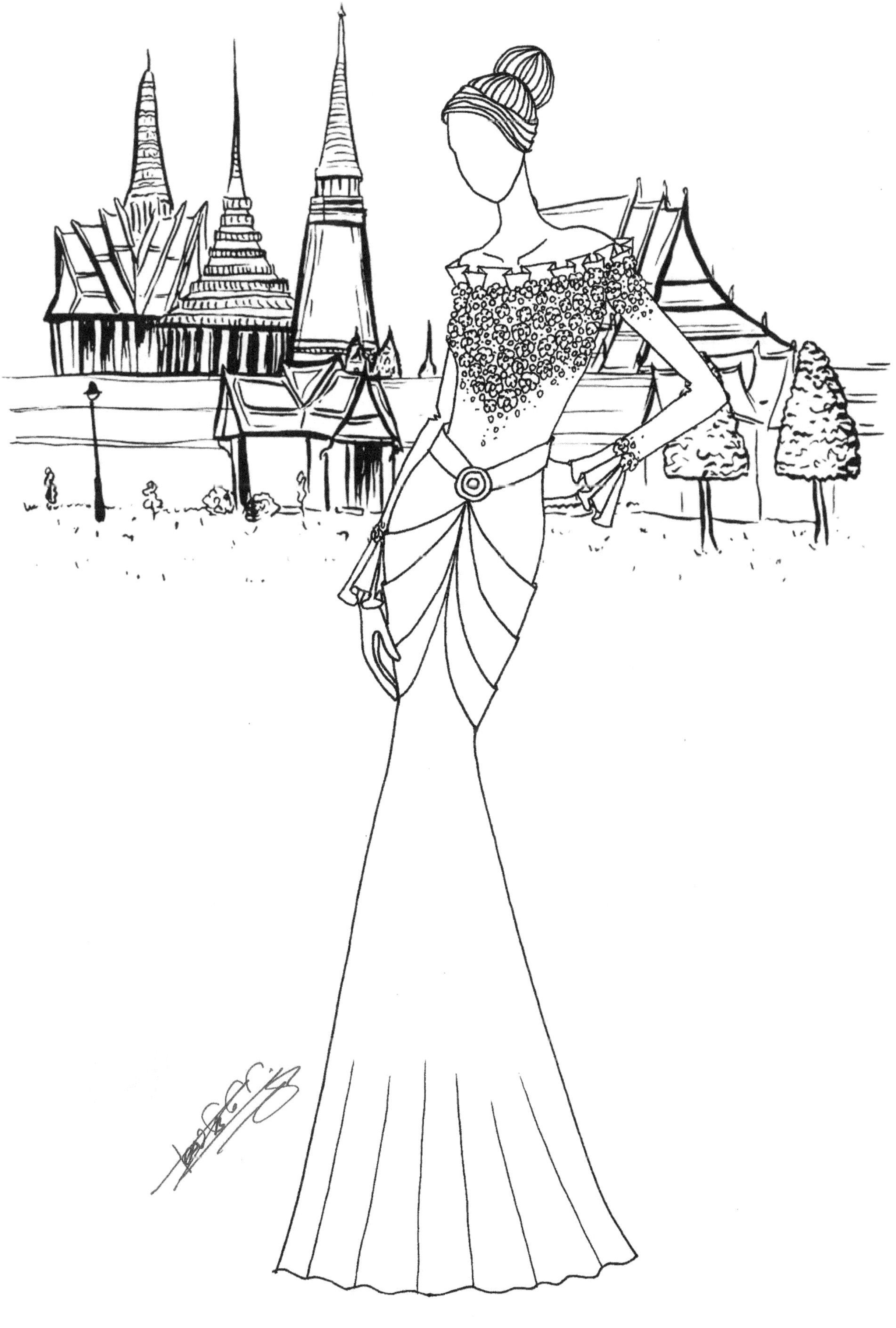

www.ingramcontent.com/pod-product-compliance
Lightning Source LLC
Chambersburg PA
CBHW081618220526
45468CB00010B/2926
* 9 7 8 1 7 2 0 5 9 1 3 4 4 *